Copyright Notice

About the Author

Jamie Brennan is a full-time Global Information Systems Programmer and a freelance Information Technology Consultant.

Chapter Overview

Chapter 1 – Introduction: The first chapter in your game design journey provides an introduction into the world of iOS and SpriteKit. You'll also learn how to set up and configure XCode for the first time.

Chapter 2 – Sprites & Nodes: Here you'll discover how to implement sprites and nodes into your very first game. You'll learn about visual effects such as rotating, scaling, and positioning.

Chapter 3 – Physics: Learn how to apply physical characteristics to nodes and see how objects on the screen can interact with each other.

Chapter 4 – Control: In this chapter, you'll discover touch screen controls, multi-touch and how to handle actions when touches begin and end.

Chapter 5 – Interactions & Gameplay: Add exciting elements to your game that will enhance the playability, challenge and fun factor.

Chapter 6 – Sound: Add some personality to your game with catchy music and sound effects. Create a continuously looping theme song for specific levels.

Chapter 7 – Scenes & Levels: Add multiple levels and scenes to your game allowing you to increase the challenge and keep the player entertained.

Chapter 8 – Particle Effects: Enhance your game by adding stunning visual effects included with SpriteKit.

Chapter 9 – Publishing & Finalizing: Add some gloss to your game and learn how to publish it in the App Store.

Preface

About "Learn SpriteKit"

This book will give you a step-by-step guide for creating a 2-dimensional game using Apple's graphics rendering framework, known as SpriteKit. Learning how to create a 2D game is the foundation for building any game, including 3D games. With the increase of the popularity in "grab and go" games, 2D games are becoming ever more relevant in the casual gaming community.

How to use this book

This book can be read from start to finish, or you can cherry pick a topic of your interest.

Each chapter contains a set of step-by-step instructions for each module. At the end of the chapter, the lessons learned are combined into the final game. If you already have an existing game, this allows you to jump to the topics that interest you the most without requiring you to read the book from start to finish.

Conventions & icons

Below describes how things will appear in the book.

Block of Code:

```
//THIS IS A COMMENT BLOCK (GREEN)
This.represents = SourceCode(code),swift
```

Quick Notes & Tips:

 A box with a light bulb contains a quick tip or optional activity for you to try out.

Customer service

Asset Files: The assets catalog is <u>not</u> required if you plan on creating your own sound and images. All of the source code, sounds, and images from this book are organized in the assets catalog to help you get up and running as quickly as possible.

Obtaining the Asset Files: A link to the asset files was included as part of the e-mail you received when you purchased this book. If you purchased a different version of this book, or if you've lost the link to the asset files, please feel free to contact 2D Game World at support@2dgameworld.com.

Table of Contents

Preface 2

Chapter 1 6

  Introduction 6

    What is SpriteKit? 6

    System Requirements 6

    Installing Xcode 7

    Creating a New Xcode Project 7

    Device Orientation 9

    Breakdown of Auto-Generated Files 9

  Nodes & Actions 11

    Nodes 11

    Actions 11

    Sprites 11

    The Parent-Child Relationship 11

    Adding a Background to our Platform Game 11

    Adding more elements to our scene 13

    Adding a Player to our Scene 17

    Creating a Texture Atlas 17

    Actions 19

    Applying Actions to the Player Sprite 19

    Rotating 19

    Animation Speed 20

    Scaling 20

    Transparency 21

    PNG Images and Transparency 22

    Default Coordinates 22

Chapter 2 23

  Physics 23

    Physics Overview 23

    Add Physics to the Player 23

Add Physics to the Environment 23

Add a Floor Node 24

Physical Property Variations 25

Chapter 3...27

Control 27

Overview 27

Detecting Touches 27

Handling Releases 30

Multi-touch 32

Better Controls 34

Chapter 4...35

Interactions & Gameplay 35

Interactions 35

Looping the ground endlessly 35

Dynamic vs. Static 36

Adding an Enemy Sprite 36

Calculating Score/Hits 37

Chapter 5...40

Sound 40

Sound Overview 40

Sounds and SpriteKit 40

Chapter 6...41

Scenes & Levels 41

Overview 41

Scenes. 41

Creating the Title Screen 41

Transitions..44

Adding a Transition to a Scene..45

Chapter 7...46

Special Effects 46

Introduction 46

Now that we've covered many of the basics, let's make your game shine with some cool effects.
SpriteKit includes a number of particle effects that simulate the appearance rain, fire, and other
elements. 46

Creating a Particle File 46

Chapter 8 48

Publishing & Finalizing 48

About Publishing 48

Submitting your App to the App Store 48

Adding a Launch Icon 48

Finalizing & Marketing 48

Acknowledgements 49

Chapter 1
Introduction

What is SpriteKit?

SpriteKit is a powerful set of tools released by Apple to allow anyone to build a game for the hugely popular iPhone, iPad, iWatch and iTV devices. SpriteKit is oriented towards 2D games, which were popular in the 80's and 90's, but have recently become hugely popular in the mobile gaming community.

Some examples of popular 2D games for iOS include Candy Crush, Hay Day, and the infamous Flappy Bird.

System Requirements

In order to run and build games effectively, you will need the following minimum system requirements:

- A Mac Computer capable of running Xcode 7
- OSX El Capitan (or newer)
- An iPhone, iPad, or other device that is capable of running iOS

Games can be fully designed and tested using your Mac computer alone; however having an iOS device, such as an iPhone or iPad will give you the best performance and overall experience. A free developer account from Apple is required to test on your iDevice – sign up at http://developer.apple.com.

Apple is famous for changing the syntax of Xcode and SpriteKit with new iterations of Xcode. It is highly recommended that you use Xcode version 7 for all of the tutorials in this book, in order to avoid problematic compilation errors.

Installing Xcode

The easiest way to install Xcode is to use the App Store from your Mac.

To install Xcode:

1. Launch the App Store
2. Download and install the latest version of Xcode
3. The download is provided by Apple and is free of charge
4. As of this writing, we are using Xcode Version 7.2 (7C68), however all of these samples should work just fine with later versions

Creating a New Xcode Project

Let's get started on your very first game! The SpriteKit SDK contains very basic game to help get you up and running.

To Create your First Game:

1. Open **Xcode**
2. Click **Create a new Xcode project**

3. In the iOS tab, ensure that **Application** is selected
4. Click **Game**

5. Click **Next**
6. Beside **Language,** ensure that **Swift** is selected
7. For the **Product Name**, enter **PlatformGame** and click **Next**
8. Select a folder to save the game, and click **Create**
9. Under **Deployment Info**, beside **Device Orientation**, <u>unselect</u> **Portrait**

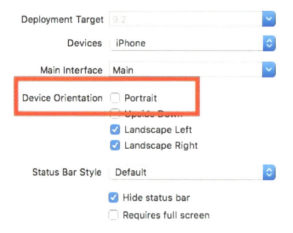

10. Beside the **Stop** button, you'll see "Platform Game". Select **iPhone 5** as the simulator, or, if you have an iPhone of your own, plug it in now.

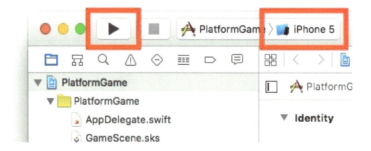

11. Press the **Play** Button

Apple's pre-built game will appear. Clicking or touching the screen will generate an image of a rotating space ship. This game is included with every new SpriteKit project.

Device Orientation

Portrait – The most common format for everyday apps, but generally not recommended for a classic 2D-style game.

Upside Down – Holding your device with the microphone facing up. This option is usually not practical.

Landscape Left – Holding the device with both hands. On some devices, the player's hand might muffle the speaker in this case.

Landscape Right – Holding the device with both hands.

Checking both **Landscape Left** and **Landscape Right** will cause iOS to automatically rotate the screen based on how the player is holding the device. This is the format we will use throughout this book.

Breakdown of Auto-Generated Files

On the left-hand side of Xcode, you'll notice that several files are created when you create a new SpriteKit project. These are the basic building blocks of every game. Let's have a look at them:

AppDelegate.swift

- Defines how your game behaves when there's an interruption, such as;
- Pressing the home button
- Receiving a phone call
- Switching to another app

GameScene.sks

- Provides an editor to design your game without any coding
- Allows a designer to visualize a scene without running the project
- Provides Live Physics Simulation

GameScene.swift

- Allows you to code every element of your scene
- You can customize/code objects added to the GameScene.sks

GameViewController.swift

- Defines level-specific items such as;
- Differentiate between a main menu, level, or cutscene

Main.storyboard

- Displays your game on the device
- Gathers information about your game and beams it onto the screen

LaunchScreen.xib

- Defines what the player will see when they first open your game
- Landscape mode, portrait and the size of the screen

Nodes & Actions

Nodes

A node can be thought of as a tool in the SpriteKit toolbox. A node is a basic element that you customize for your game. Nodes can include the following:

- Moving or Static Images
- Labels
- Shapes
- Lighting Effects
- Camera Movement
- Audio

Actions

Nodes can be manipulated and customized by assigning the **SKAction** object to the node. For example, assigning an **SKAction** to a player node will allow you to move him left or right. Assigning an **SKAction** to a sound node will allow you to modify special audio effects or stop the stop audio completely.

Sprites

A sprite can be simply defined as any computerized image that is moved around on the screen. Your player is a sprite and other objects on the screen such as enemies and obstacles are also considered sprites. Sprites use the **SKSpriteNode** object and movement is achieved using the **SKaction** object.

The Parent-Child Relationship

The **GameScene** class is the parent and its children are all of the nodes contained within it.

Adding a Background to our Platform Game

We're going to add our very first node to our scene, a background image.

1. Open the Platform Game that we created in **Chapter 1**
2. Using the **Assets** from **Chapter 1**, drag and drop **background.png** into the project
3. Accept all the defaults when prompted, and click **Finish**
4. Highlight and replace all of the code that appears after the **didMoveToView** function in the **GameScene** class. The code is highlighted in light blue below:

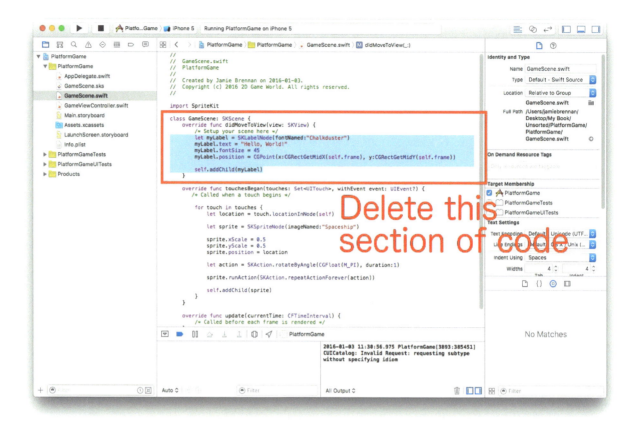

5. Replace the code, so it appears as follows:

```swift
import SpriteKit

class GameScene: SKScene {
    override func didMoveToView(view: SKView) {

        let Sky: SKSpriteNode

        Sky = SKSpriteNode(imageNamed: "background")

        //place the image in the center of the screen
        Sky.position = CGPoint(x:CGRectGetMidX(self.frame), y:CGRectGetMidY(self.frame))

        self.addChild(Sky)
    }

}
```

The following image will appear on your screen:

Adding more elements to our scene

Our background sky looks a little boring, so let's add some clouds and trees to the scene.

1. Using the **Assets** from **Chapter 2**, drag and drop **clouds.png** into the project
2. Open **GameScene.swift**
3. Add the following lines of code to the existing code:

```swift
import SpriteKit

class GameScene: SKScene {
    override func didMoveToView(view: SKView) {

        let Sky: SKSpriteNode
        let Clouds: SKSpriteNode

        Sky = SKSpriteNode(imageNamed: "background")
        Clouds = SKSpriteNode(imageNamed: "clouds")

        //place the image in the center of the screen
        Sky.position = CGPoint(x:CGRectGetMidX(self.frame), y:CGRectGetMidY(self.frame))
        Clouds.position = Sky.position

        self.addChild(Sky)
        self.addChild(Clouds)
    }
```

}

4. Repeat these steps, adding the **Trees** and **Mountains:**

```swift
import SpriteKit

class GameScene: SKScene {
    override func didMoveToView(view: SKView) {

        let Sky: SKSpriteNode
        let Clouds: SKSpriteNode
        let Mountain: SKSpriteNode
        let Trees: SKSpriteNode

        Sky = SKSpriteNode(imageNamed: "background")
        Clouds = SKSpriteNode(imageNamed: "clouds")
        Mountain = SKSpriteNode(imageNamed: "mountain")
        Trees = SKSpriteNode(imageNamed: "trees")

        Sky.position = CGPoint(x:CGRectGetMidX(self.frame), y:CGRectGetMidY(self.frame))
        Clouds.position = Sky.position
        Mountain.position = Sky.position
        Trees.position = Sky.position

        self.addChild(Sky)
        self.addChild(Clouds)
        self.addChild(Mountain)
        self.addChild(Trees)
    }

}
}
```

5. Open **GameViewController.swift**
6. Highlight the following code:

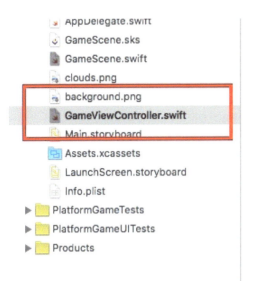

```
//
// Created by Jamie Brennan on 2016-01-03.
// Copyright (c) 2016 2D Game World. All rights reserved.
//

import UIKit
import SpriteKit

class GameViewController: UIViewController {

    override func viewDidLoad() {
        super.viewDidLoad()

        if let scene = GameScene(fileNamed:"GameScene") {
            // Configure the view.
            let skView = self.view as! SKView
            skView.showsFPS = true
            skView.showsNodeCount = true

            /* Sprite Kit applies additional optimizations to improve
            skView.ignoresSiblingOrder = true

            /* Set the scale mode to scale to fit the window */
            scene.scaleMode = .AspectFill

            skView.presentScene(scene)
        }
    }
}
```

7. And replace it with:

```
skView.ignoresSiblingOrder = false
```

Setting the **ignoresSiblingOrder** flag to **false** will allow us to strategically place each node in the z-order of our choice. It's not as fast as letting the computer decide where to place each element, but we'll focus on further optimizing our game later on in the book.

8. Now run your project, and you'll have a nicely set up scene with a sky, trees, and mountains.

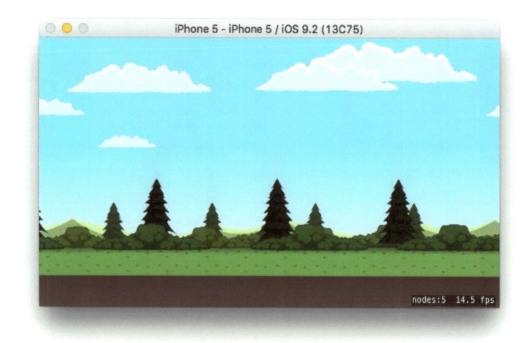

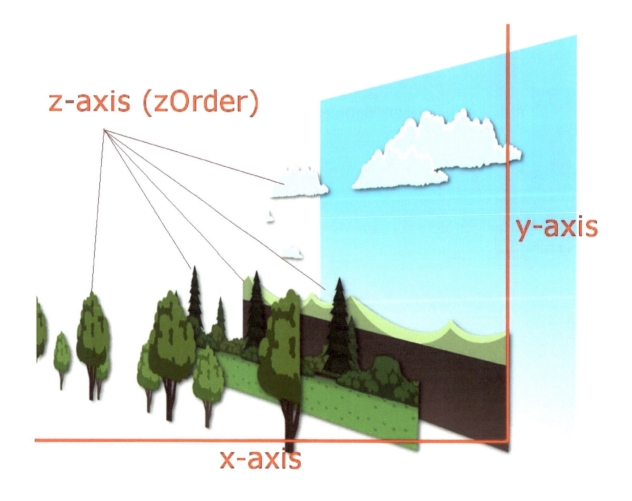

Each node will be added to the scene in the order it we specified in the code.

Adding a Player to our Scene

Now that our game is becoming more complete, it's time to add a player sprite to our scene.

1. Open **GameScene.swift**
2. Below the **GameScene: SKScene** class, enter the following code:

```
let PlayerAtlas = SKTextureAtlas(named:"player.atlas")
var PlayerSprites = Array<SKTexture>()
var Player = SKSpriteNode()
```

3. Now, in the **didMoveToView** function, enter the following code:

```
PlayerSprites.append(PlayerAtlas.textureNamed("player1"))
PlayerSprites.append(PlayerAtlas.textureNamed("player2"))

Player = SKSpriteNode(texture:PlayerSprites[0])
Player.position = CGPoint(x:CGRectGetMidX(self.frame), y:CGRectGetMidY(self.frame));

addChild(self.Player)
```

4. There's still one step left before running our game - we need to create a texture atlas.

Creating a Texture Atlas

A texture atlas is a series of images bundled together to make our game more organized and run more efficiently. We're going to create a Texture Atlas for our player sprite to that will allow us to animate him.

1. In **Finder,** create a new folder called **player.atlas**
2. Using the **asset files** from **Chapter 2,** copy **player1.png** and **player2.png** into the **player.atlas** folder
3. Drag and drop the **player.atlas** folder into Xcode

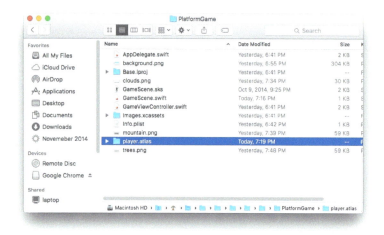
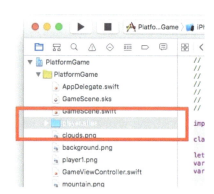

4. Now, run your project. You'll see a player in the middle of the screen, standing still.

 Can't see your player? He might be hiding behind the trees! Check the **addChild** order and make sure the player sprite is the last node added to the scene.

Actions

Actions provide gameplay to your game. Without actions, you would simply have a static picture rendered on your device's screen.

Typical actions include:

- Changing the position of a node
- Making the node bigger/smaller
- Applying animation
- Rotating a node
- Playing audio
- Destroying a node

Applying Actions to the Player Sprite

Let's apply an action to the player sprite. For this action, we are going to animate our player by flipping through different images and then repeating the action using the **repeatActionForever** method.

1. Open **GameScene.swift**
2. In the **didMoveToView** function, enter the following code:

```
let PlayerWalk = SKAction.animateWithTextures(self.PlayerSprites, timePerFrame: 0.2)
let repeatAction = SKAction.repeatActionForever(PlayerWalk)
self.Player.runAction(repeatAction)
```

3. Now run the code. You'll see that your player is now animated. But he's still floating in mid-air. In the next chapter, we'll apply physics to change this behaviour.

Rotating

```
rotateByAngle:duration
```

Rotating a node will allow you to spin the node in either clockwise or counter clockwise for a given duration.

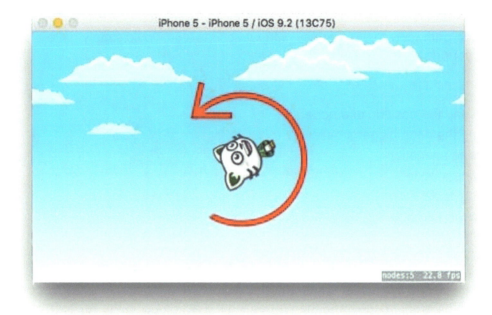

Animation Speed

`speedBy:duration`

Changing the animation speed will affect how quickly different sets of images (such as images contained in a Texture Atlas) are displayed.

Scaling

`scaleBy:duration`

Scaling an image for a particular duration will allow you to change this size of an object by making it progressively bigger or smaller.

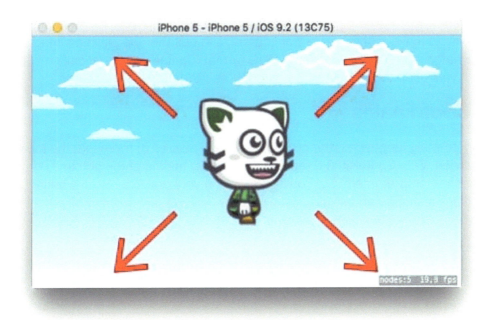

Transparency

`fadeInWithDuration:duration`

Transparency changes the ability to "see through" a node. This effect is great for ghosts!

PNG Images and Transparency

The easiest way to make a sprite semi-transparent is to edit the *opacity* in an image editor such as GIMP or Photoshop and saving it in the PNG format. SpriteKit automatically recognizes images with levels of opacity and makes it appear "see-through" on the screen.

Default Coordinates

In many programming languages, the coordinates zero, zero (0,0) represent the top-left hand side of the screen. With SpriteKit, 0,0 represents the very middle of the screen. This may sound funny to seasoned programmers, but you'll find that it's very practical when working with several devices of different shapes and sizes.

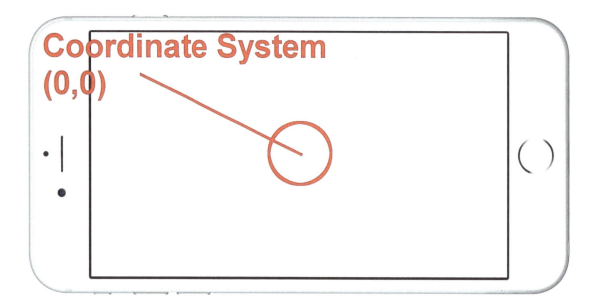

Chapter 2
Physics

Physics Overview

Physics, much like real-life physics give our environment a sense of reality by adding unseen forces such as gravity, motion, and impulses. Elements such as water and wind will affect cause will have a different effect on an object and can be applied accordingly.

SpriteKit comes with everything you need to apply physics to your game.

Add Physics to the Player

A player without a physics body will make for a very boring and predictable platform game. Let's add some physical properties to our player:

1. Add the **SKPhysicsContactDelegate** protocol to our **GameClass** scene. Don't forget to add a comma after **SKScene**:

```
class GameScene: SKScene, SKPhysicsContactDelegate {
```

2. In the **didMoveToView** function, enter the following code:

```
Player.physicsBody = SKPhysicsBody(rectangleOfSize: CGSize(width: Player.size.width, height: Player.size.height))
```

3. Run your game

Did you catch what happened when you ran your game? The player fell right through the bottom of the screen. This is the intended effect for now. What has happened is the player now has physical properties, but the environment doesn't. The player is no floating around endlessly in space, so let's give our environment some physical attributes as well.

Add Physics to the Environment

Collisions are the basis for platform games. A collision occurs when a node comes into contact with another node and reacts to it in some fashion, just like a ball bouncing when it hits the floor.

Let's make the edges around our screen solid, causing a collision between the player and the borders of the screen.

1. In the **didMoveToView** function, enter the following code:

```
self.physicsBody = SKPhysicsBody(edgeLoopFromRect: self.frame)
```

2. Run your code. Your player will now fall to the bottom of the screen.

Add a Floor Node

Let's create a floor node for the player to land on:

1. Add the **floor.png** image to your project
2. Below the **GameScene: SKScene, SKPhysicsContactDelegate** class, declare a variable for the floor:

```
var Floor = SKSpriteNode()
```

3. the **didMoveToView** function, create an anchorPoint to line everything up:

```
view.scene!.anchorPoint=CGPoint(x: 0.5, y: 0.5)
```

4. Again in the **didMoveToView** function, enter the following code:

```
let Floor: SKSpriteNode
Floor = SKSpriteNode(imageNamed: "floor")
Floor.physicsBody = SKPhysicsBody(edgeLoopFromRect: Floor.frame)
Floor.position = CGPoint(x:CGRectGetMidX(self.frame), y:-220)
self.addChild(Floor)
```

5. Run your game. The player will now land on the floor you've just added to the scene.

Just for fun: add the following lines of code to see the player bounce up and down across the screen:

Player.physicsBody!.friction = 0.0
Player.physicsBody!.restitution = 1.1

We'll re-visit these properties shortly!

Physical Property Variations

SpriteKit provides several different options for assigning physics bodies to your nodes.

| bodyWithCircleOfRadius | bodyWithRectangleOfSize | SKTexture |

The most efficient physical property is the circle-based body. The least efficient is the texture-based body, because the computer must perform complicated calculations around your sprite. In most cases, the circle and rectangular-based bodies will be appropriate for your game.

Physical property attributes can be customized using SpriteKit to ensure that your player acts appropriately to its surroundings. A player swimming around in an underwater world would behave much more different than a player skating on an ice rink.

Here are a few supported physical property attributes included with SpriteKit:

Mass – defines the weight of an object. This affects momentum.

Density – Related to mass, and defined in kilograms. When you change the mass, the density is adjusted for consistency.

Friction – Defines how smooth/bumpy a surface is. You can adjust the friction to simulate sliding on ice, or walking on a bumpy rural road.

Restitution – The bounciness of an object. A ball would be very bouncy, whereas a bag of potatoes would just fall to the ground.

LinearDamping – This is similar to having wind forcing an object in a particular direction.

AngularDamping – Similar to *LinearDamping*, but affects all directions instead of a straight line. Great for underwater levels.

Chapter 3
Control

Overview

When Steve Jobs introduced the iPhone, many people were horrified at the thought of a touch-screen interface. Why? Because the touch screen is dynamic and buttons are never in the same place at once. This works to our advantage in a platform game.

Detecting Touches

In a platform game, touch controls should be placed in convenient places, such as the bottom of the screen, and should not interfere with the visibility of important objects and the player.

Let's add a control to our project that will make our player node jump:

1. Add the **button.png** image to your project
2. Below the **GameScene: SKScene, SKPhysicsContactDelegate** class, declare a variable for the floor:

```
var Jump:SKNode = SKSpriteNode(imageNamed: "button")
```

3. In the **didMoveToView** function, add the following code for our **Jump** button

```
Jump.position = CGPoint(x:350, y:-220)
self.addChild(Jump)
```

4. Time to get rid of the spaceship that came with Apple's sample game – select and delete the code highlighted (in blue) below:

```
override func touchesBegan(touches: Set<UITouch>, withEvent event: UIEvent?) {
    /* Called when a touch begins */

    for touch in touches {
        let location = touch.locationInNode(self)

        let sprite = SKSpriteNode(imageNamed:"Spaceship")

        sprite.xScale = 0.5
        sprite.yScale = 0.5
        sprite.position = location

        let action = SKAction.rotateByAngle(CGFloat(M_PI), duration:1)

        sprite.runAction(SKAction.repeatActionForever(action))

        self.addChild(sprite)
    }
}

override func update(currentTime: CFTimeInterval) {
    /* Called before each frame is rendered */
}
}
```

5. Within the **touchesBegan** function, and below the **location** declaration, we're going to add an **if** statement that will determine if the **Jump** button we just added was touched:

```
if self.Jump.containsPoint(location)
{
    self.Player.physicsBody!.applyImpulse(CGVectorMake(1, 500))
}
```

6. Run your code and click/touch the button that appears on the right. Your character will jump up in the air!

The **applyImpuse** method pushes our character up in the air using the built-in physics engine. Play around with the CGVectorMake numbers to see the difference in impulses.

Now let's add a left and right button to further control our player:

7. Drag and drop **left.png** and **right.png** into your project
8. In the the **GameScene: SKScene, SKPhysicsContactDelegate** class, declare a variable for the **MoveRight** and **MoveLeft**:

```
var MoveRight = SKSpriteNode()
var MoveLeft = SKSpriteNode()
```

9. In the **didMoveToView** function, enter the following code to display and position our left and right buttons:

```
MoveRight = SKSpriteNode(imageNamed: "right")
MoveRight.position = CGPoint(x:-240, y:-220)

MoveLeft = SKSpriteNode(imageNamed: "left")
MoveLeft.position = CGPoint(x:-390, y:-220)
addChild(self.MoveRight)
addChild(self.MoveLeft)
```

10. Now, assign an action to the left and right buttons to make the player move in the correct direction within the **touchesBegan** function, and below the **location** declaration:

```
if self.MoveRight.containsPoint(location)
{
```

```
        let moveRight = SKAction.moveByX(200, y:0, duration:1)
        let repeatAction = SKAction.repeatActionForever(moveRight)
        self.Player.runAction(repeatAction, withKey: "MovingRight")
}

if self.MoveLeft.containsPoint(location)
{
        let moveLeft = SKAction.moveByX(-200, y:0, duration:1)
        let repeatAction = SKAction.repeatActionForever(moveLeft)
        self.Player.runAction(repeatAction, withKey: "MovingLeft")
}
```

11. Run your game. By touching the right and left buttons, you will see that your player will start walking in that direction. Stop and start your game to test left and right.

Handling Releases

We don't want our player to open and close our game every time just to make the player walk back and forth. Let's clean up our code by adding functions to detect when the user released a the button.

1. In the Below the **GameScene: SKScene, SKPhysicsContactDelegate** class, declare a variable to detect if the player is jumping, moving and what the last button pressed was:

```
var isTouching = false
var isJumping = false
var lastButton = "none"
```

2. Return to the code in the **touchesBegan** function. Delete the existing code and replace it with the following simplified functions:

```
if self.MoveRight.containsPoint(location)
{
        MovePlayerRight()
        lastButton = "right"
}
if self.MoveLeft.containsPoint(location)
{
        MovePlayerLeft()
        lastButton = "left"
}
if self.Jump.containsPoint(location)
{
        isJumping = true
        MakePlayerJump()
}
```

3. Now, let's create a function for our newly created shortcuts:

```
func MovePlayerRight()
{
isTouching = true

    if isTouching
    {
    self.Player.removeActionForKey("MovingLeft")
    let moveRight = SKAction.moveByX(200, y:0, duration:1)
    let repeatAction = SKAction.repeatActionForever(moveRight)
    self.Player.runAction(repeatAction, withKey: "MovingRight")
    }
}

func MovePlayerLeft()
{
isTouching = true

    if isTouching
    {
    self.Player.removeActionForKey("MovingRight")
    let moveLeft = SKAction.moveByX(-200, y:0, duration:1)
    let repeatAction = SKAction.repeatActionForever(moveLeft)
    self.Player.runAction(repeatAction, withKey: "MovingLeft")
    }
}

func MakePlayerJump()
{
    if isJumping
    {
    self.Player.physicsBody!.applyImpulse(CGVectorMake(1, 500))
    }
}
```

4. Now, let's create another function to detect when touches have ended by adding the **touchesEnded** function:

```
override func touchesEnded(touches: Set<UITouch>, withEvent event: UIEvent?) {
    for touch: AnyObject in touches {

let location = touch.locationInNode(self)

    if !self.MoveRight.containsPoint(location) && isTouching == false
    {
    self.Player.removeActionForKey("MovingRight")
    }

    if self.MoveRight.containsPoint(location)
    {
    self.Player.removeActionForKey("MovingRight")
    }
```

```
        if !self.MoveLeft.containsPoint(location) && isTouching == false
        {
        self.Player.removeActionForKey("MovingLeft")
        }
        if self.MoveLeft.containsPoint(location)
        {
        self.Player.removeActionForKey("MovingLeft")
        }
        if self.Jump.containsPoint(location)
        {
        self.Player.removeActionForKey("Jump")
        }
    }
}
```

5. Run your game. You will now see that the player is much more easily controlled.

Whew, that was a lot of coding! The good news is these functions can be re-used throughout your game and do not need to be touched again.

Multi-touch

In most cases, you're going to want to be able to press multiple buttons at one time – especially with a platform game where many actions take place, such as walking and jumping or shooting a projectile all at once. This is where Multi-touch comes in to play.

Let's add multiple touch abilities to our game by adding the **touchesMoved** function:

1. Add the **touchesMoved** function:

```
override func touchesMoved(touches:Set<UITouch>, withEvent event: UIEvent?) {

for touch in touches {
let location = touch.locationInNode(self)
}
}
```

2. Within the **touchesMoved** function, enter the following code:

```
if self.MoveLeft.containsPoint(location)
{
        if lastButton == "right"
        {
        MovePlayerLeft()
        }

        self.Player.removeActionForKey("MovingRight")
```

```
        lastButton = "left"
        isTouching = true
}

if self.MoveRight.containsPoint(location)
{
        if lastButton == "left"
        {
        MovePlayerRight()
        }

        self.Player.removeActionForKey("MovingLeft")

        lastButton = "right"
        isTouching = true
}

if !self.MoveRight.containsPoint(location) && !self.MoveLeft.containsPoint(location)
{
        isTouching = false
}
```

3. Now run your project. You can now jump and walk at the same time!

Good job! We've covered a lot of new functions in this chapter.

Adding or subtracting to the 200 within the **moveRight** variable will allow your player's speed to increase or decrease.

Better Controls

The best way to add control to your game is to cover an entire portion of the screen, instead of just the area of the button. This will provide correction in the case that the player moves his finger slightly off of the button area.

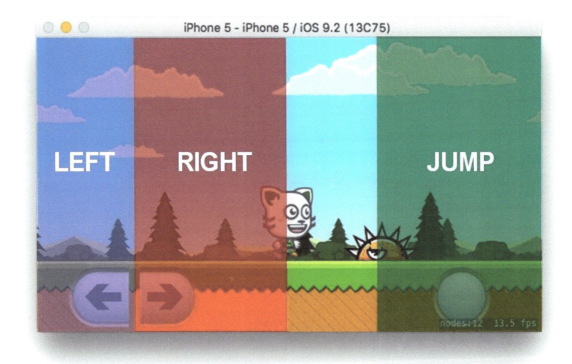

Chapter 4

Interactions & Gameplay

Interactions

Every game needs some form of interaction with the world around it. Your player needs to be able to respond to objects on the screen.

Looping the ground endlessly

Looping is an important part of many 2D games. You want to be able to loop a set of trees, the ground, and other objects endlessly to avoid having a huge image that comes to a halt.

Note: Before continuing, remove all references to the **Floor** node (except the asset image), as we will no longer be using it.

Let's create a ground loop:

1. In the the **GameScene: SKScene, SKPhysicsContactDelegate** class, declare a variable for the floor:

```
var Floor1 = SKSpriteNode()
var Floor2 = SKSpriteNode()
```

2. In the the **didMoveToView** function, declare an **SKSpriteNode** for the floor:

```
Floor1 = SKSpriteNode(imageNamed: "floor")
Floor2 = SKSpriteNode(imageNamed: "floor")
```

3. Now, let's create a physics body for the floor and prevent it from being a dynamic object:

```
Floor1.physicsBody = SKPhysicsBody(rectangleOfSize: Floor1.size)
Floor2.physicsBody = SKPhysicsBody(rectangleOfSize: Floor1.size)

Floor1.physicsBody?.dynamic = false
Floor2.physicsBody?.dynamic = false
Floor1.position = CGPoint(x:CGRectGetMidX(self.frame), y:-220);
Floor2.position = CGPointMake(Floor1.size.width-1, -220);
```

4. As usual, we need to add the floor to the scene using the **addChild** method:

```
addChild(self.Floor1)
addChild(self.Floor2)
```

5. In the **update()** function, we will create an if statement to continuously loop the floor when the edges of the floor meet:

```
Floor1.position = CGPointMake(Floor1.position.x-5, Floor1.position.y);
Floor2.position = CGPointMake(Floor2.position.x-5, Floor2.position.y);

if (Floor1.position.x < -Floor1.size.width){
        Floor1.position = CGPointMake(Floor2.position.x + Floor2.size.width, Floor1.position.y);
        }

if (Floor2.position.x < -Floor2.size.width) {
        Floor2.position = CGPointMake(Floor1.position.x + Floor1.size.width, Floor2.position.y);
        }
```

This is a useful function that you will find yourself using throughout your entire game design career!

 To view an outline of collision objects, add skView.showsPhysics = true to your **GameViewController**

Dynamic vs. Static

Having a **dynamic** physics body will allow an object to move around on the screen. This means that if the object collides with another object, it will move according to whatever type of physical characteristics has been assigned to it. Having a **static** physics body will keep the object in place on the screen, preventing it from moving around.

Adding an Enemy Sprite

Now we're going to add an monster to our game.

1. Using the Assets from Chapter 5, drag and drop **monster.png** into the project
2. In the the **GameScene: SKScene, SKPhysicsContactDelegate** class, declare a variable for the monster sprite

```
var Monster = SKSpriteNode()
```

3. In the the **didMoveToView** function, set up the properties for the monster node:

```
var Monster = SKSpriteNode()
Monster = SKSpriteNode(imageNamed: "monster")
Monster.physicsBody = SKPhysicsBody(rectangleOfSize: Monster.size)
Monster.position = CGPointMake(self.frame.width, -115);
Monster.physicsBody?.dynamic = false
```

4. Now add the monster to the scene using the **addChild** method:

```
self.addChild(Monster)
```

5. In the **update()** function, add a simple loop to make the enemy appear:

```
Monster.position = CGPointMake(Monster.position.x-5, -115);

if (Monster.position.x < -Monster.size.width * 4) {
   Monster.position = CGPointMake(self.frame.width, -115);
}
```

Calculating Score/Hits

Now you need to make the game challenging. If you hit the enemy, you will lose life.

1. First we need to create a collision mask, to allow our code to differentiate different collisions:

```
enum collisionType:UInt32 {
    case player = 1
    case monster = 2
}
```

2. Now we'll declare a label to display on the screen, as well as an energy integer:

```
var energyLabel = SKLabelNode(fontNamed: "Arial")
var intEnergy = 10
```

3. In the **didMoveToView** function, add the **contactBitMask** properties as follows:

```
self.physicsWorld.contactDelegate = self

Player.physicsBody?.categoryBitMask = collisionType.player.rawValue
Player.physicsBody?.contactTestBitMask = collisionType.monster.rawValue

Monster.physicsBody?.categoryBitMask = collisionType.monster.rawValue
Monster.physicsBody?.contactTestBitMask = collisionType.player.rawValue
```

4. Set the position and label for the Energy Label Node:

```
energyLabel.text = "Energy: " + String(intEnergy)
energyLabel.position = CGPointMake(CGRectGetMidX(self.frame), 200)
energyLabel.fontColor = UIColor.blackColor()
energyLabel.fontSize = 50
```

5. Now add the **LabelNode** using the AddChild routine:

```
addChild(self.energyLabel)
```

6. Now we're going to create a function called didBeginContact and populate it with collision detection:

```
func didBeginContact(contact: SKPhysicsContact) {

    let bitMask = contact.bodyA.categoryBitMask | contact.bodyB.categoryBitMask
```

```
    switch(bitMask)
    {
    case collisionType.player.rawValue | collisionType.monster.rawValue:
        intEnergy = intEnergy - 1
        print("Player has hit enemy")

        if (intEnergy > 0)
        {
            energyLabel.text = "Energy: " + String(intEnergy)
        }
        else
        {
            energyLabel.text = "GAME OVER!"
            self.Player.removeFromParent()
        }

    default:
        return
    }

}
```

When the player's energy runs out, you will be presented with a "Game Over" message!

Chapter 5
Sound

Sound Overview

A game is simply not complete without sounds. Background music adds atmosphere to a level. Action sounds, such as the player jumping or hitting an object create a feeling of realism. Luckily, adding sounds couldn't be easier with SpriteKit.

Sounds and SpriteKit

Before Apple released iOS9, programmers were forced to use an external library and include it with their project. Now, SpriteKit includes an extremely powerful sound tool in the form of the **SKAudioNode** object. Now, in less only 3 lines of code you can have background music playing in a continuous loop!

1. Using the Assets from **Chapter 6**, drag and drop **music.wav** and **jump.wav** into the project.
2. Below **import SpriteKit,** add two variables, background and jump sounds

```
let backgroundMusic = SKAudioNode(fileNamed: "music.wav")
let jumpSound = SKAudioNode(fileNamed: "jump.wav")
```

3. Add the child node, just like the image nodes:

```
addChild(self.backgroundMusic)
```

4. In the MakePlayerJump() function, add the code highlighted below:

```
func MakePlayerJump()
    {
    if isJumping
    {
    self.runAction(SKAction.playSoundFileNamed("jump.wav", waitForCompletion: false))
    self.Player.physicsBody!.applyImpulse(CGVectorMake(1, 500))
    }
}
```

That's it! It's really that easy to add sounds to your project!

Chapter 6

Scenes & Levels

Overview

Every game needs to have a variety of challenges and levels. In this chapter, we will create a title screen and shift it right into the gameplay. We will demonstrate how to have multiple levels to increase the challenge and keep the player engaged.

Creating the Title Screen

1. Click **File / New / New File…**
2. Select **iOS** and click on **Swift File** and **Next**
3. Save the file as **TitleScreen** and click **Create**
4. Click **File / New / New File…**
5. Click **SpriteKit Scene** and click **Next**
6. Save the file as **TitleScreen** and click **Create**
7. From the **Assets Catalog** for **Chapter 7,** drag and drop **title.png** to the project
8. Click on the **GameScene.swift** file
9. Create a reference to a (non-existent at this point,) title screen class below **import SpriteKit**:

```
var titleScreen : TitleScreen?
```

10. Now, create a function that will bring us to the main menu:
11. Return to your **didBeginContact** function and delete the following lines of code:

```
func showTitleScreen()
{
    titleScreen = TitleScreen(size: self.size)
    titleScreen!.anchorPoint = CGPoint(x: 0.5, y: 0.5)
    titleScreen!.scaleMode = .AspectFill
    self.view?.presentScene(titleScreen)
}
```

```
func didBeginContact(contact: SKPhysicsContact) {

    let bitMask = contact.bodyA.categoryBitMask | contact.bodyB.categoryBitMask

    switch(bitMask)
    {
    case collisionType.player.rawValue | collisionType.monster.rawValue:
        intEnergy = intEnergy - 1
        print("PLAYER HAS hit enemy")

        if (intEnergy > 0)
        {
            energyLabel.text = "Energy: " + String(intEnergy)
        }
        else
        {
            energyLabel.text = "GAME OVER!"
            self.Player.removeFromParent()
        }
    default:
        return
    }

}
```

12. Replace the code highlighted above with the following function call:

```
showTitleScreen()
```

13. Click on the **TitleScreen.swift** file
14. Add the following lines of code below **import Foundation:**

```
import SpriteKit

var level1Scene : GameScene?

class TitleScreen: SKScene {

var title = SKSpriteNode()

    override func didMoveToView(view: SKView) {

    view.scene!.anchorPoint=CGPoint(x: 0.5, y: 0.5)

    title = SKSpriteNode(imageNamed: "title")
    title.size = self.size
    title.size.height = self.size.height - 190

    addChild(self.title)
}

    override func touchesBegan(touches: Set<UITouch>, withEvent event: UIEvent?) {
```

```
            level1Scene = GameScene(size: self.size)
            level1Scene!.anchorPoint = CGPoint(x: 0.5, y: 0.5)
            level1Scene!.scaleMode = .AspectFill
            self.view?.presentScene(level1Scene)
        }
    }
```

15. Run your game
16. Now you can see that when you hit a game over, you are returned to a Title Screen.

17. Naturally, you would want the title screen to appear *before* the game begins. Let's do that by opening **GameViewController.swift:**

43

```
import UIKit
import SpriteKit

class GameViewController: UIViewController {

    override func viewDidLoad() {
        super.viewDidLoad()

        if let scene = GameScene(fileNamed:"GameScene") {
            // Configure the view.
            let skView = self.view as! SKView
            skView.showsFPS = true
            skView.showsNodeCount = true

            /* Sprite Kit applies additional optimizations to improve rendering
            skView.ignoresSiblingOrder = false

            /* Set the scale mode to scale to fit the window */
            scene.scaleMode = .AspectFill
```

18. Replace the code in the image above with the following code:

```
if let scene = TitleScreen(fileNamed:"TitleScreen") {
```

Congratulations! You now have a title screen and can add multiple levels.

Transitions

Transitions provide a dramatic visual effect when moving from one scene to the next. SpriteKit includes the following transitions by default:

Crossfade

Horizantal Open

Verticle Open

Doors Open

Doorway

Fade with color

Fade with duration

Flip Horizontal

Flip Verticle

Move in with a direction

Push in a direction

Scenes & Levels

Reveal

Check out 2DGameWorld's YouTube channel to see a demo of every single transition included with SpriteKit!

Adding a Transition to a Scene

1. In the **GameScene.swift** scene, go to your showTitleScreen() function and update the existing code so that it appears as follows:

```swift
func showTitleScreen()
{
titleScreen = TitleScreen(size: self.size)
titleScreen!.anchorPoint = CGPoint(x: 0.5, y: 0.5)
titleScreen!.scaleMode = .AspectFill
let MyTransition = SKTransition.fadeWithColor(SKColor.redColor(), duration: 4)
self.view?.presentScene(titleScreen!, transition: MyTransition)
}
```

Chapter 7
Special Effects

Introduction

Now that we've covered many of the basics, let's make your game shine with some cool effects. SpriteKit includes a number of particle effects that simulate the appearance rain, fire, and other elements.

Creating a Particle File

1. In Xcode click **File / New / File**
2. Below **iOS**, select **Resource**
3. Select **SpriteKit Particle File** and click **Next**
4. Select **Rain** and click **Next**
5. For the name enter **RainParticle** and click **Create**
6. You will now see a file called **RainParticle.sks** and **spark.png** added automatically to your project in Xcode

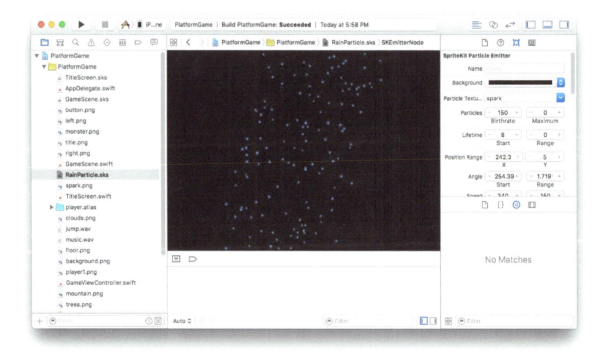

7. Play with the settings on the right
8. Below **import SpriteKit** define the particle

```
var RainParticle = SKEmitterNode(fileNamed: "RainParticle")
```

9. Now add the following code:

```
RainParticle?.setScale(4)
RainParticle?.position.y = 300
self.addChild(RainParticle!)
```

10. You'll now have a snow flakey effect as per the screen image below:

Default Particle types:

- Bokeh
- Fire
- Fireflies
- Magic
- Smoke
- Snow
- Spark

Chapter 8
Publishing & Finalizing

About Publishing

So now you've created your masterpiece and it's time to share it with the world. **Where do you start?**

Apple has made it incredibly easy for independent (or indie) developers to publish their game sin the App Store. Anyone with a Mac and Xcode and publish their game with ease. At the time of this writing, there is a cost of about $100 to become registered an Apple Developer. This is small price to pay for the amount of attention your app will receive. iOS is the most popular operating system in the world, and has the most devices in gamer's hands than any other.

Submitting your App to the App Store

Once you've completed your game, it's time to send it to Apple for review.

1. Sign up for an Apple ID
2. Click on the Project Name
3. Click the **General** tab, if necessary
4. Enter a **Bundle ID**. This is a unique identifier for your App. The default is usually acceptable
5. For the **Signing Identity,** select Mac App Store
6. Follow the on-screen directions to submit your App.

Adding a Launch Icon

The icon you create is the image that will appear on the launch screen of you iOS device. By default, the icon is a plain white image with black circular lines.

1. Click on the Project Name
2. Select the drop-down for **App Icons and Launch Images**
3. Drag and drop an icon into the project navigator

Finalizing & Marketing

Finally, when you have finished your masterpiece, it's time to market your game. The best way to market your game (as of 2016) is Facebook. Get your game out there by placing an ad or video of the gameplay. Start with a meme to attract niche group of interested people.

Acknowledgements

Graphics

Seargent Cat by Spoggles (educationalfunforkids.com). Licenced under Creative Commons: By Attribution 3.0. http://creative commons.org/licences/by/3.0

Audio

Pixelland Kevin MacLeod (incompetech.com). Licensed under Creative Commons: By Attribution 3.0. http://creative commons.org/licences/by/3.0

Jump by soundnimja (freesound.org). Licensed under Creative Commons: By Attribution 3.0. http://creative commons.org/licences/by/3.0

support@2dgameworld.com

Twitter: @2dgameworld

Facebook: www.facebook.com/2dgameworld

Web: www.2dgameworld.com